RAJEEV MUDUMBA

THE PODCAST CHECKLIST

A book on creating, launching & growing your ideal podcast!

THE PODCAST CHECKLIST

BY

RAJEEV MUDUMBA

Table of Contents

The PLAN B SUCCESS Journey

When I was able to find some time between jobs, I decided to create something that leveraged my decades of expertise, skills and experiences in business & life. The idea of Plan B Success was born!

The next few weeks went into researching the world of podcasting and its evolution over time. I felt it an opportune time to start one. While there are over 750K podcasts on the largest platform for podcasts, Apple Podcast alone; statistics show that only a couple of hundred thousand are truly active and a few hundred produce and grow consistently. And, the listenership is on a steep growth curve with the attention span in the 80% range. There is no greater place to be, to impact and benefit the most number of people while building a following and creating an influencer base.

While there are several podcasters in every niche, very few create and deliver quality content. In the niche I had chosen around business, entrepreneurship, education and training; there were several churning out episodes of interviews with entrepreneurs and other inspirational players in various domains. But, very few produced well-researched and organic personal & business growth content that would benefit an audience of entrepreneurs, professionals and students. With what I could deliver, this was a perfect opportunity!

The next step was to learn everything there is around podcasting and deliver a stellar show in Plan B Success podcast. I immersed myself into the experience and it has been the most rewarding yet!

Plan B Success podcast is a 3 episodes a week podcast where every Monday, I release an interview with an inspiring personality to share nuggets of information from their journey which may benefit the listeners. The other two episodes, released on Wednesday and Friday are content I develop based on topics I choose or sought by listeners to benefit them in their journey to success.

On July 15th 2019, I launched Plan B Success podcast. Very quickly, it climbed the ranks of the best-rated podcasts in its space in several countries. Most importantly, it provides immense value to students, professionals and entrepreneurs in their personal and professional growth journey.

At the same time, it's a rewarding experience for me as a podcaster to be able to make new connections and savor opportunities that come my way as a result of reaching out to others.

I have one question for you! What would it mean to you if you embarked on a journey to increase your reach, grow your brand and influence and benefit several out there with what you have to share and say?

I created this podcast checklist to help you reach your goal of starting a podcast quickly without the hours of research that I spent on. First, understand what podcasting is about and the benefit it provides to your audience as well as you and then, let's touch upon every aspect you need to be prepared with to launch an awesome show!

Why is there not a better time than NOW to Podcast?

1. *Give your voice a platform*

You are a sum total of your skills, talents & experiences in life. You have a story and a message to share and the world needs to know, to draw inspiration from you, your story and your message. With the rapid growth of consumption of podcasting as an audio media, now is the opportune time to create and grow it. It also helps cement your personal or professional brand and brings opportunities your way that you did not dream of.

2. *Competition is yet to take off*

While there are millions producing video content and blogs, the total number of podcasts sits at around 750K on Apple Podcast, the largest platform for podcasts. Of these about a few thousands are active and producing content regularly. The awareness around podcasting has also risen sharply in recent years with about 60+ million dialing into an average of 8 podcasts and listening to them attentively about 80% of the time.

With such a great attention span, you will attract listeners to your message.

3. *Network with your audience and guests*

Podcasts range from solo episode where you can pick a topic and talk about it with your audience directly to episodes where you interview guests. You have the ability to reach the common man or the most influential celebrity directly to be a guest on your podcast. Imagine the networking opportunities you have at hand to meet and know people personally and the ability to turn them into business opportunities.

4. *Enjoy an influential relationship with your listeners*

Podcasts help position you to have intimate relationships with you listeners as you have their complete attention. You can become an influencer par excellence as a result and benefit your listeners through multiple opportunities of engaging them. You could engage them through courses, content and other ways. The most important aspect of a thriving relationship with your listeners is to engage with them authentically and in full transparency. This will ensure that your message resonates with them and they will take note.

5. *Grow your business*

By increasing your brand value as a result of podcasts, you can avail multiple opportunities to grow your current business. If you don't have one, you can setup a business and offer multiple value opportunities to your listeners. From partnering with your guests to speaking sessions, from offering consulting to your listeners to creating products and services for them, it's a fertile ground for growth. Finally, you will also learn a lot from your guests and listeners in this journey. You will be a better human being as well as a better entrepreneur/ businessperson. I can vouch for this through my own experience and the growth of Plan B Success podcast!

Your Podcast Roadmap

Let's jump into this workbook to help you crystallize your thoughts as you make decisions about your podcast. This will allow you to create and grow the best podcast possible so you reap the rewards down the line...

1. **What is my podcast about? What niche do I want to focus on?**

Take stock of your skills, expertise, talents & interests and answer this question. You should pick a niche that you will enjoy in the long term. Podcasting is about clarity and consistency. You need to be prepared for the long run. So, choose wisely!

Example: Plan B Success is a resource full of inspiring and though provoking personal and business development content & interviews with inspiring personalities to benefit Entrepreneurs, Professionals and You!

2. **Who are my listeners?**

Who do you want to attract to listen to your podcast and your message? Who do you want to engage constantly and provide value for? Spend quality time determining your customer avatar. What I mean by this is that you get granular about who you want to appeal to? This is important to get fixated upon since you have to create content consistently to drive value to this customer avatar and the listeners will be engaging with you and your brand directly. They seek to learn from you and benefit from it.

Example – Plan B Success customer is the 18-65 individual, at school or at a job looking to create alternate avenues of personal and professional growth and entrepreneurs seeking new ways of growing their business.

3. How will your listeners benefit?

Listeners seek to find value in your content and benefit from it. Else, they will lose interest and search for value elsewhere. You need to ascertain the needs of your customer avatar and ensure that all your content is to fulfill their needs. Understand their problems and pain points. From time to time, seek them out to hear from them as to what their issues are and what they need. You may not have all the answers but you can be on a constant mission to find them and share what you find with your listeners.

Example: Plan B Success is focused on content that helps the listeners improve their personal growth, professional growth at work and business growth for entrepreneurs. This includes tools, tips and tricks to ensure they make progress in the direction they seek. You can check out a few episodes on Plan B Success podcast to understand what I described here.

4. **Why should listeners stick with your podcast when there are others out there? What is your unique value or selling proposition (USP)?**

This is an important question to answer. You can go to any of the podcasting platforms and check the podcasts out there in your specific niche. Do this research and review a few of their episodes. Learn what each of them offers as a USP to retain and grow their audience. List out 10 podcasts and their USP according to you.

Now, determine how you will differentiate your podcast from them in terms of offering unique value.

Note - At a later point, you could reach these podcast hosts to partner on content or invite them as guests on your podcast while you feature on theirs.

Example: Plan B Success podcast is a 3 episode a week podcast where one episode pertains to interviewing an inspiring personality while the other two are topic specific content that I deliver for the listeners. My USP is the value I provide with these topics while all the other podcasts out there in the realm are about interviews only.

#	Podcast Name	USP
1		
2		
3		
4		
5		
6		
7		
8		
9		
10		

The best way to do this is to be in the shoes of your listener and ask yourself why you would want to listen to your show. Now, what's your USP?

Podcast Strategy

1. How many episode should I publish each week?

The short answer is at least 1 a day, but that may not be practical as you need to research and create your content and all aspects of podcast creation take time. In order to delivery quality over quantity, you can decide on at least 3 to 1 episode a week. History has shown that those with an episode a week have grown faster in terms of listenership as they have fresh content every day. Plan B Success podcast, as I shared earlier does 3 episodes a week, releasing on alternate working days.

2. What should be the length of each episode?

This is up to you. Average length is about 30-45 minutes since that has shown to keep listeners engaged. What's important is to keep the listeners engaged by providing them value in your content consistently. Sometimes, longer episodes may dilute content and fail to keep listener attention. Other times, you need the time to discuss a topic at length. You could start out with shorter episodes and as you get good at your craft, plan on the ideal size of your episodes.

As with everything, practice helps hone your skill and make you better.

3. **How do I plan each episode and publishing strategy?**

Just like anything in life, planning goes a long way in creating and managing an efficient podcast. If you are planning on interviews for your podcast, you will need time and energy to arrange for them, record them, edit them, create cover art for them and then, upload them. All this takes time. Based on the frequency of your content creation and episodes timeline, my recommendation would be to plan this process and create your episodes weeks to a month before they will be released. This means that you should plan to produce and keep ready episodes worth a few weeks to a month beforehand, upload them in batches and while they get released per a schedule, you can focus on preparing for future episodes and promoting your podcast.

The ideal timeframe is to be 3-4 weeks ahead in the game. In some cases where the topics are current in nature, you may need to record and upload at opportune times.

Take a stab below at planning for your first 10 episodes of your podcast. You know, topics you want to focus on, guests you want to invite, etc.

Episode #	Topic	Guests	Notes
1	Introduction of yourself and the show to new listeners. Make suretogivepeople anideaofwhythey should subscribe, and what they have to look forward to.		
2			
3			
4			
5			
6			
7			
8			
9			
10			

Checklist

This is a podcast checklist and a shorter version to my comprehensive podcasting eBook All You Need To Know About Podcasting. It will guide you through each and every essential step along the path toward creating your first podcast.

Resolve Before You Start Podcasting

Podcasting is a continuous journey. Its exciting and a great learning experience. Consistency is the key. Resolve to be disciplined and put in the work needed to groom it into a great podcast, a resource that listeners depend on for entertainment, for learning and more. By consistently delivering quality content, you will reap great rewards in the future of your podcasting career!

X	Commitment
	I'll launch my podcast on _____.
	I'll upload ___ episodes every week/month
	I'll make a list of all the things I learn and enjoy in the process during the first 12 months

	I'll remind myself of these goals and stick with it even when I feel low.
	I'll NOT GIVE UP!

First Five Things to Decide On

X	Important Decisions to Manage Your Brand
	Your Podcast Title:
	Your Podcast Sub Title:
	Your Podcast Description:
	Your Host Name:
	Your Podcast Cover Art/ Logo: (1400 x 1400 pixels minimum, 3000 x 3000 pixels maximum; RGB colors)

Tools & Technology for Your Podcast

Editing Software:

- GarageBand is free with Mac computers and is easy to use.
- Audacity is free software and does a wonderful job, not just for beginners but for the established as well.

Below are some of the best equipment choices that you may choose from based on your budget.

Microphones:

- Samson Meteor Mic USB Studio Microphone (Chrome) Bundle With SR350 Stereo Headphones (76.99)
- Blue Yeti Condenser USB Microphone, Blackout ($110.00) or Blue Yeti Nano Premium USB Microphone ($92.50)
- Mudder Microphone Foam Windscreen Microphone Covers for Blue Yeti, Yeti Pro Condenser Microphone, 3 Pack ($6.99)
- Rode smartLav+ Omnidirectional Lavalier Microphone for iPhone and Smartphones ($57.50)

- Audio-Technica ATR2100-USB USB/XLR Microphone with Knox Pop Filter and Headphones ($89.99)

Equipment needed for recording in-person interviews:

You would need a smartphone along with a USB Camera Adapter (Apple Lightning to USB Camera Adapter ($29.99)) to record video along with audio using Zoom H6 Recorder.

- Recorder: Zoom H6 Six-Track Portable Recorder ($329.99)
- Shure SM58-LC Cardioid Dynamic Vocal Microphone Bundle with Stand Adapter and Zipered Pouch ($129.95)
- **Microphones:** A pair of Audio-Technica ATR3350IS Omnidirectional Condenser Lavalier Mic with Smartphone Adapter ($29.00)
- TISINO 1/4 Mono to 3.5mm Stereo Adapter, Gold Plated 6.35mm TS Male Plug to 1/8 Inch TRS Female Audio Connector – 2 Pack ($9.99)
- Headphone Splitter Cable, Gold Platted ($8.85)
- Duracell Rechargeable AA Batteries – 4 count ($8.99)
- Duracell Fastest Value Charger with 4 AA Batteries 1 Kit ($21.99)
- Energizer LR44 1.5V Button Cell Battery 20 Pack ($6.66)

Headphones:

You may use your regular smartphone ear pods with a microphone. However, investing in a good pair of headphones will last you longer and work better. Here are a few options for you.

- Sony MDR7506 Professional Large Diaphragm Headphone ($89.88)
- Audio-Technica ATH-M20x Professional Studio Monitor Headphones ($49.00)
- Audio-Technica ATH-M30x Professional Studio Monitor Headphones ($69.00)

Software needed for recording remote interviews over the Internet:

If you plan on doing remote interviews or have more than one person join a podcast from across the globe, you can use any of the following remote recording software solutions to connect and record your content episodes. Ensure you record in a quiet room and ask your guests to do the same on their end so sound is captured in the best quality possible.

- Squadcast.fm ($20.00/month) – This is a great solution to record remote interviews professionally. It records in lossless WAV format and ensures separate tracks are recorded locally for each guest and the host. This results in impeccable audio quality, HD video, up to 3 guests backed by customer friendly support.

- Zencastr ($20.00/month) – This is a similar solution like Sqadcast, however it doesn't allow for video recording.

- Skype & Zoom are other solutions that you may start with to get familiar with remote interview recording. The free versions of either allow this. I have used both and like Zoom better since it allows for full video screen recording of the one speaking while Skype divides the screen between the host and guest. The audio quality also is better with Zoom though, not as good as SquadCast. You can separate audio tracks while recording in Zoom to get a tad better audio quality. With a paid version, you can do more with settings in these kinds of software.

How to record and export your episodes before your upload

- Keep your mouth at least a foot away from the microphone to get the best sound while you speak.

- Ensure your recording levels are set where they do not go into the red when you speak.

- Only record as long as you want the episode to be, focus on delivery of value.

- With every episode, introduce your show and what the episode is about.

- At the end of your episode, have a call to action instructing your listeners to do something; perhaps to subscribe and leave a review for your podcast.

- Weave the listener experience with other modes of content you have through the show notes, whether a blog or video that they can visit.

- While editing, focus on noise reduction and clarity.

- Export your episode as an .mp3 file onto your computer.

- Tag your file with ID3 tags, which will be requested by your editing software before saving. This includes your title, host name, release date, genre, year, etc.

Hosting your podcast

- Subscribe to a podcast hosting service such as LibSyn, Anchor, SoundCloud, PodBean or another. They provide you with space to house your podcast content. A hosting service provider stores your podcast content including podcast cover art, podcast description, content episodes, episode specific cover art, show notes and tags.

- They may give your own website as well.

- Upload your episodes to the hosting service. It will walk you through the steps of uploading your .mp3 file, your cover art, show notes, tags etc. before you schedule release.

- You can create blog posts with your episodes embedded on your blog and other social media for promoting them.

- Decide on the podcast platforms you want your show on. The prevalent ones with large listener bases are iTunes or Apple Podcast, Google Play, Spotify, SoundCloud, Stitcher, TuneIn, RadioPublic, Pandora and you can even push your episodes to YouTube. Most of them will allow you to showcase your podcast for free. **Focus on** Apple Podcasts, Stitcher, **&** Google Play. **Use the links to setup your podcast on these platforms.** Here's how to submit your podcast to Apple.

There you go! You are ready to roll now with your own podcast!!

Launch your podcast and focus on promoting it on all your social media, your friends and family and climb the ranks of the "New and Noteworthy" for Apple Podcast in the first 8 weeks. This will bring a lot of organic traffic your way and help you grow your listenership.

Podcasting can open doors to opportunities for you and your business that you may not have dreamed of. Leverage the most efficient branding tool out there and of course, do get back in touch if I can be of any service!

Here's to your success!

About the Author

Rajeev Mudumba is a dynamic entrepreneur, executive, business strategist, coach, and advisor. He is also an accomplished author, speaker and thought leader and a die-hard optimist.

Throughout his professional life, Rajeev has built profitable, value-based businesses, nurtured strategic partnerships and built lifelong friendships. He has worked with organizations and individuals to remedy challenges and achieve results. Rajeev has achieved stellar results in international business, new business lines, and now, is focused on helping you succeed in your profession and/ or business and get the most out of your life.

Rajeev hosts an award-winning popular podcast, Plan B Success where he shares insightful and thought-provoking personal and business growth strategies and interviews inspiring entrepreneurs and professionals. He is also the creator and coach of two coaching programs: Plan B Success REVEAL (focused on helping you meet your true authentic self) and Plan B Success BLUEPRINT (focused on enabling you learn the creative and technical aspects of launching your own online coaching business). All the information is available on Rajeev's website.

Rajeev also speaks and writes frequently on the topics of personal and professional growth, self-empowerment, life & career coaching among others. He has recently launched his book "My Inspiration: Quotes that shaped my self improvement journey" which is available on Amazon. Rajeev has delivered several keynote/ topical speeches at national & international conferences. He has made it his mission to extract from his experiences and share value to mentor individuals, current/ future entrepreneurs and executives, startups, scale-ups, and large corporations.

Accolades include World Affairs Council of Kentucky and Southern Indiana's 2010 Global Visionary Award, Business First of Louisville's Forty Under 40 Award, Telehealth and Medicine Today's 2016 Publisher's Award & Indian Achievers Forum's 2017 Indian Achievers' Award for Healthcare and Education.